The Self-Confidence Factor:

A Parent's Guide to Bully Prevention

By
Sifu Karl Romain

Contents

4

Testimonials

"Training with Sifu Karl Romain has helped boost my confidence and focus in many facets of my life. It helped give me the courage to tackle obstacles head-on, and I'd recommend this book to anyone who needs their own confidence boost."
John Francis Daley, Black Belt, writer and actor (Dr. Sweets on "Bones")

"With specific techniques for building mental resilience and physical strength, The Self-Confidence Factor is a wonderful tool for both parents and kids trying to deal with conflict in a productive way. This book provides the skills and discipline to handle any situation."
Lisa Oz, Author and radio and television personality

After reading "The Self-Confidence Factor, A Parent's Guide to Bully Prevention," I thought to myself, "Finally! A much needed resource that approaches the issue of bullying from a different perspective than other books I've read regarding bullying". This book addresses the issue of bullying with the approach that you, the parent, can take a proactive role in giving your child the tools they need to be better able to handle themselves when confronted by a bully. "The Self-Confidence Factor" provides parents and caretakers with the information they need to provide their child with the greatest defense against bullying, CONFIDENCE. The book should be read by all parents and caretakers of elementary school age children.
Greg N., Former law enforcement officer with 28 years experience

My son was going to a new school where he didn't know anyone. The kung-fu training gave him confidence to introduce himself to other kids. This led to him participating in the playground activities. One incident he discussed with me was about a child known to bully others. This bully charged towards my son, he used a simple technique he learned in kung- fu that directed the bully in another direction. He felt empowered which allowed him later to stand up for a new student who was being picked on. The self-confidence factor is extremely important.

Karen Marchione, Parent and Educator

Dedication

This book is dedicated to the young people everywhere who have suffered at the hands of bullies, and to the families that suffer along with them. It is my sincere hope that the ideas I present here serve to put an end to bullying situations and teach parents and children ways to work together to avoid those situations in the first place.

In my continuing effort to help children live happy and healthy lives, a portion of the proceeds from the sales of this book will be donated to The DON'T WAIT Project® and Healthcorps®. (See the Resources Section at the end of this book for more information.)

In loving memory of Sheryl Chasin who supported my efforts in bully prevention.

Acknowledgements

I would like to offer a special thanks to the Cajucom family for being a part of this book. I would also like to thank the following people: John Francis Daley, Lisa Oz, Greg N, Karen Marchione, Amy Barone, Lisa Bradshaw, Charles Elion, the staff and students of Edgewater Kung-Fu. Special thanks to Sandra Klein for all her help in publishing this book.

Foreword

As a former NFL football player (Philadelphia Eagles, '67-'70), who comes from a family of athletes, I wanted my five-year-old daughter, Ashley, to participate in some kind of competitive sport. Her mother wanted her to be a ballerina, wearing pretty little tutus. Of course, I went along willingly with her desires, but was amazed to find out that Ashley wasn't too fond of being a ballerina. That gave me an opportunity to suggest other activities.

I had noticed, while playing make-believe softball with her at home, that she had very good coordination. She loved hitting the ball and running around the kitchen table for a home run. I could see that she had talent.

When I was introduced to Sifu Romain, who was a Master in Kung Fu and ran a Martial Arts Academy, he invited me to become a student. I told him I would think about it, but that I would like to enroll my daughter.

I decided to enroll Ashley in Sifu Romain's Kung Fu Academy in Edgewater for a number of reasons. As a football player, I knew that to be successful in anything you have to prepare, because success is only realized when "preparedness meets opportunity;" and I believed that training in Kung Fu would help to prepare her for any number of activities by strengthening her self-confidence and focus while teaching her self defense.

Another concern I had was a growing pattern of "bullying" in our schools. I wanted my daughter to have the kind of confidence that would be displayed in the way she walked, talked, and behaved — to be respectful and polite, but with a fearless attitude, and a feeling she could control any given situation.

All of this was realized when I enrolled Ashley in Edgewater Kung Fu. I noticed another element being taught; that I felt was rather unique— public speaking. The kids were speaking for 20 to 30 seconds on any topic of their choice. For example, their favorite ice cream, TV programs, songs, their favorite story book, their baby sister or brother. I thought, "What a tremendous way to build confidence in a child!"

There are adults who are terrified to face a crowd, and this aspect of the training convinced me that I had my daughter in the right place, in the right school, with the right instructors to prepare her for all the things the world would present to her.

From the day she received her White Belt, her dreams and aspirations were to one day get her Black Sash. Today, Ashley has her 2nd Degree Black Sash.

She is a talented teenager with big dreams and goals, and the self- confidence to achieve them. She has accomplished this with the support and involvement of her parents and the life lessons learned from martial arts and leadership training.

Sifu Romain's book, "The Self-Confidence Factor: A Parent's Guide to Bully Prevention," is a practical tool for parents, educators, and childcare providers who are in need of tools that will assist them with the bullying epidemic in our communities today. I am also convinced that this book will help develop, and send into the world, some of our future leaders. I have taught Ashley to always remember that, "Everything we do or say in our lives every day has a consequence, and where we find ourselves today is the result of what we've done before."

Chuck Elion, Former Philadelphia Eagle

Preface

I chose to write this book because, as a martial arts instructor with more than 20 years of teaching experience, I have noticed an increase in the number of children attending my academy because they are being bullied in school. Parents are working and stressed out trying to work and care for their family. Teachers have to deal with overcrowded classrooms and curriculum standards. Frustration is growing.

Most of the children being bullied are not getting the help they desperately need. We hear that teen suicides and violence are on the rise. Hopefully, this book can provide some necessary tools and answers for parents, children, and educators alike.

Bullying is at epidemic proportions in our communities. Statistics show that:
• 1 out of 4 kids is bullied.
• 1 out of 5 kids admit to being a bully, or doing some bullying.
• A daily average of 160,000 children miss school because they fear they will be bullied if they attend classes.
• On average, 282,000 students are physically attacked by a bully each month.
• Every 7 minutes, a child is bullied on a school playground, with more than 85% of those instances occurring without any intervention.

The numbers are disturbing. In cases of playground bullying, peer intervention occurred in just 11% of cases, while adults intervened only 4% of the time!

I have also noticed that parents who were bullied themselves are seeking the help and answers that they didn't receive when they were children. Most are still dealing with the effects of bullying, even as adults. Without intervention, bullying can impact a victim's future life in many insidious ways, including problems forming close relationships, problems with asserting oneself, issues with self-confidence, and poorly developed tolerance for frustration.

I have seen how teaching such important life skills as communication, public speaking, and rapport building have improved the confidence level of my students. I can remember one student in particular who was struggling with not only being bullied, but also with his ability to make friends. This child had a lot of great qualities but was shy and socially awkward. His parents hoped that learning martial arts would make a difference. It did on a physical level, but it still wasn't quite enough to bring out the qualities in him that we all knew he had. This challenged me to take a closer look at what I was doing.

Martial arts teaches students more than just how to improve their physical stamina, speed, and coordination. I wanted to know why it wasn't enough to bring this boy out of his shell. As I continued to work with him, I realized that he wasn't alone. Adults had some of the same issues.

That's when we changed our focus from being a black belt school to becoming a black belt leadership school.

We began teaching leadership skills in conjunction with the martial arts techniques and philosophy that we have always used. When we analyzed the results of our new programs, we saw a tremendous improvement across the board in the confidence level of our students. That's when I realized the true value of the Confidence Factor.

13

The child I mentioned above not only got the bullies to leave him alone without ever getting into a physical altercation, but also quickly became much more popular with his peers. He went on to know that he could handle himself in any situation, and that's real confidence. He learned that he could handle himself if things got physical, but more importantly, he learned to first use his verbal skills as a tool to help him make friends and defuse confrontations.

That kind of success is why I am so compelled to share what I have learned through my experiences. I have approached this subject of bullying from the perspective of both life skills and martial arts. Together, they can develop the Confidence Factor for any student that applies themselves.

It is my sincerest wish that you will explore and use the information contained in this book. This subject is of such grave importance to our children's lives and the quality of our communities. I am confident that by using these techniques, huge benefits will be reaped by children, communities, and schools everywhere.

Before You Begin . . .

1. This book is focused on giving parents the tools necessary to help their children develop confidence and overcome bullying. Read the book all the way through. Then re-read it a second time, making notes along the way.

2. Now it's time to apply what you have learned. Please be deliberate in using what you have learned. This is a great opportunity for you to bond with your child, so make it fun!

3. Use the questions at the end of each chapter to investigate your child's experience. Keep asking questions to get the whole story.

4. Role-play everything! This is the only true way to measure what your child has learned.

5. Seek the help of a professional where it is needed. However, you are the most important factor in your child's progress. Your involvement is critical to their success.

Introduction

Bullying is nothing new, but the extent that it goes to today, makes the effects far worse than they have been in the past. Tragically, it is not uncommon for anxiety and depression to be exacerbated by bullying to the point where teens — and even younger children — commit suicide.

When one of these tragic teen suicides occurs, the associated news story almost always reports that bullying was a serious component in the factors that caused the young person to be in such distress. Kids today are not only subject to being pushed around at school or on the streets, but now they have to contend with online attacks — which can be much more difficult to deal with.

The Suicide Prevention Resource Center reports that both victims and bullies are at a higher risk for suicide than their peers. Some children are bullies and are themselves bullied by others. Studies have found that they are at the highest risk for suicide.

Parents, guardians, and educators all want to keep children safe, but we can't always be with them, and we certainly won't know what is going on in the virtual world unless we know what to look for and how to go about it.

Teaching kids how to defend themselves physically is a big part of what a martial arts instructor does, but the most important part of self defense is not actually in the techniques. Does it surprise you to hear that from a martial arts instructor?

Self defense is fundamentally non-physical in that it begins with understanding how to interact with other people in a positive way, avoiding behaviors and situations that encourage aggression from others, and knowing what to do before trouble escalates to a physical confrontation.

The importance of the mental and psychological aspects of self defense does not diminish the importance of martial arts training, though. Children, especially, do not have any experience with taking charge of a situation. The confidence and skills they gain from training in the martial arts will position them to succeed in applying the non-physical techniques that will be taught in this book.

In the following chapters we are going to cover several different types of bullying, ways to defuse situations, what to expect from (and require of) school officials, ways to work with your children to best support and protect them, and of course, show you the basic self defense techniques taught in our martial arts program.

This book is intended to provide information, but also to be a guide to navigating the challenges of your particular situation. Take the time to answer the discussion questions at the end of each section. They are designed to engage you and help you see how to apply the material for the maximum benefit to the children in your care.

Chapter 1: What Is Bullying?

Bullying is any hurtful behavior that is intentional, repetitive, and ongoing. It can involve physical abuse, verbal abuse, threatening behavior, or social humiliation.

Deliberately trying to harm or humiliate others is the main characteristic of a bully. This behavioral pattern causes a lot of problems for the one on the receiving end of the bullying. These actions of intimidation allow the bully to always be in a position of power.

Studies have shown that bullies are made, not born. Therefore, when detected at an early age, it is possible to train a child to control bullying impulses.

Basic bullying behavior may include verbal or written abuse or exclusion from activities and social situations, as well as physical abuse. Bullies behave this way to be perceived as popular or tough, or to get attention.

Bullying can be classified into two categories:

1. Physical aggression
2. Social aggression

Examples of physical aggression include: shoving, poking, choking, punching, kicking, hair pulling, scratching, and biting.

Examples of social aggression include: spreading gossip, refusing to socialize with the victim, bullying other people who wish to socialize with the victim, criticizing the victim's race, religion, disability, or sexual orientation.

Characteristics of Bullies
Research indicates that adults who bully have a strong need to control. Some bullies reflect the environment of their childhood home, repeating what they learned from their parents. Researchers have identified that the characteristics of a bully include: quickness to anger, addiction to aggressive behaviors, perceiving others' actions as hostile, and engaging in obsessive actions.

Although bullying behavior has its origin in childhood, behavioral patterns become more sophisticated as a bully ages. Schoolyard pranks and "rough- housing" can develop into more elaborate schemes. Planned attempts to discredit the victim's character, or less obvious yet equally forceful forms of coercion, are possible.

Think of such attempts as social terrorism: The bully seeks absolute dominance over his or her victim and will use whatever means are most convenient — or emotionally gratifying — to gain it. Bullies may spread rumors designed to make the target unpopular. They may play ugly pranks to get a laugh and do emotional or physical damage to the victim. They may create elaborate schemes to put their victims in a humiliating position.

Remember the movie Carrie? The gang of bullies that tormented the title character during the prom scene is a perfect example of the kinds of schemes that bullies are capable of.

Whichever means a bully chooses to use, the ultimate goal is the same: to terrorize the victim and the victim's peers, into acknowledging the bully's "superiority." In other words, bullies hurt others to gain what they don't have — self-confidence.

Of course, when Carrie was released in the late 1970s, bullying was limited to the schoolyard and the bus route home. Today, it is a whole new ballgame — due to the popularity of the Internet and social networking sites, the taunting and tormenting continues even when the victim is at home.

In fact, according to I-Safe, an organization dedicated to Internet safety education, 42% of children have been subjected to online bullying. Of those children, 58% have not told their parents.

Most bullies are very careful thinkers. They are prone to pick on individuals who lack assertiveness and project fear. Bullies identify the most suitable target before making their move.

Some bullies eventually change their behavior as they mature. However, some continue to be overly-assertive and unable to rationalize things in a civil manner, thus becoming a threat to society.

Discussion Questions
1. What is a bully?
2. What is the difference between physical and social aggression?
3. What are the characteristics of bullying?

Chapter 2: Cyber-Bullying—What Parents Need to Know and What They Can Do About It

Children are all too often the most vicious of all age groups. Bullying has long been a social ill in our society which only fairly recently has been taken seriously. Since the Internet and mobile Web have become a part of our lives, bullies have brought bullying into these areas as well. Commonly called "cyber-bullying," bullying by electronic communication is a serious, yet often dismissed problem. However, it is no less damaging than traditional bullying; in fact, it may be worse.

In this section, we will identify cyber-bullying and its tactics, expose misconceptions about cyber-bullying, and provide statistics to show the risk of exposure. We will also show the results of cyber-bullying on its victims, signs that your child may be a victim, and what you as a parent can do to stop the abuse. Overall, this information will arm you with what you need to know to protect your children and teens from this form of abuse.

What Parents Need to Know About Cyber-Bullying
Cyber-bullying is using electronic media such as cell phone texting, voice messaging, instant messaging, e-mail and social websites such as Facebook and Twitter to threaten, harass and harm others. It is often included as a part of a larger abusive situation. Many bullies perceive or excuse their actions as "just joking," and many bullying situations may very well have started that way. This way of thinking extends into cyber-bullying.

How Cyber-Bullying Works

Tactics of cyber-bullying include a variety of non-physical attacks which, on the most basic level, include spreading gossip and sending hateful messages.

Cyber-bullies may also impersonate someone the victim trusts to trick the victim into revealing damaging secrets so they can reveal them in order to humiliate the target. This ability to impersonate anyone can also be used to trick the victim into embarrassing situations. Bullies may even pretend to be the victim in order to turn their friends and peers against them.

Another cyber-bully favorite tactic is posting embarrassing pictures and videos of the victim, or at least making them about the victim. If the cyber- bully feels like it, they might use Photoshop to make ordinary pictures into a humiliation or an insult. Web communities such as various subgroups on Reddit or 4chan are full of such images.

As innovations are made in electronic communication and electronic media, cyber-bullies will also have access to the new technology and will use it for bullying in new and possibly more damaging ways.

Statistics of Potential Cyber-Bullying Exposure

These are some eye-opening statistics on just how much teens — and even younger children — are at risk online:
• 95-100% of teens regularly access the Internet
• 85-90% of parents think they are knowledgeable about their children's online lives
•70-75% of teens say parents stop checking at about 14 years old
•65-70% say friends sharing private pictures is a problem
•60-65% say parents know nothing about what they do online
•55-60% do not tell parents when they are bullied online

23

•40-45% say they knowingly give out personal information online
•30-35% have or are willing to meet "online friends" in real life

What is truly revealing is the difference between the percentage of parents that think they know their children's online life (85-90%) and the percentage of kids who say their parents do not know (60-65%) and even worse, how many children do not tell their parents if they are being bullied (55-60%). There is a huge gap between what parents think they know and what is actually happening.

The Effects of Cyber-Bullying on Its Victims
Just how serious is cyber-bullying? It can perhaps be more serious than traditional bullying, simply because the victim can learn to anticipate and avoid confrontations in person. Online, it is not so easy.

As the goal of some forms of bullying is maximum exposure of the victim being humiliated, the Internet and social sites are especially harmful since the exposure may not simply be among friends and peers, it can be global. The victim may feel that there is nowhere they can go to avoid the abuse. The fact that the harassing media is viewable 24 hours a day, 7 days a week also causes victims to feel anxious that at any moment, someone is harassing them.

They may lose trust in their friends, family, and peers because of impersonation tactics. Their friends and other people may also come to dislike the victim for something an impersonator said or did online. Social isolation takes on a whole new level when it is being done online.

All of these potential outcomes of cyber-bullying can lead to even more severe problems, including growing up to be a dysfunctional adult, drug and alcohol addiction, school shootings and suicide.

What Parents Can Do About Cyber-Bullying
Now that you know how cyber-bullying works and what damage it can do to your children, you need to know two things.

• First, you need to know how to tell if your child is being bullied online.

• Second, you need to know how to stop it. The signs of this kind of abuse are not as obvious as physical bullying, but are similar to social and verbal bullying.

Know the Signs of Cyber-Bullying
• Avoiding friend and peer activities
• Not attending school
• Falling or extremely fluctuating grades in school
• Isolating themselves in their rooms
• Increased unexplainable anger, resentment, or mood swings
• Self-destructive behavior such as cutting themselves
• Morbidity, fascination with violence, weapons and   death

These behaviors may not be "tell-tale" signs, but they are definitely worth your attention and concern. Some parents may write them off as typical developmental issues or "teenage angst." Regardless of this possibility, it is better to be safe than sorry. The risk to your child's welfare is too great to ignore and expect that it will pass.

Actions to Take

At this point, you may have become aware that your child is being bullied, or at least you have sufficient suspicion that it is happening. What you need to know now is how to stop the cyber-bullying and prevent it from happening again. Here are a few tips to help you.

• **Realize that you are probably not as "tech-savvy" as your kids.** You may not be as aware as you think you are as to what's going on in their digital world. Make every effort to improve your cyber-literacy and keep tabs on their online activity.

• **Take an interest in their online world**. Ask them about what has happened online as well as when they were at school or out with friends. They are less likely to tell you about cyber-bullying if you do not seem interested in their Internet activity.

• **Talk to them about cyber-safety**. Doing things such as accepting random friend requests, giving out personal information online, sexting or sharing compromising pictures and videos all expose them to the risk of cyber-bullying. One only has to read the comments on any number of YouTube videos to see this.

• **If they tell you that they are being bullied online, take them seriously and be sympathetic**. Ordinary bullying is often dismissed by parents as "toughening you up," and it can be much easier to blow off cyber-bullying. Assure them that the bully or bullies are the ones in the wrong, and that the problem is not hopeless.

• **Ask them if this is a part of a larger problem.** If they are being bullied in person when they are away from home, "easy solutions" such as flagging the online attacks as abusive or inappropriate or reporting the bully's account to the website's admin can escalate the other problems. If the cyber-bullying is part of a larger problem, consult school officials or the police about bullying. Never, ever confront the bullies or their parents directly.

• **Teach children not to respond to the cyber-bully's attack.** That is playing directly into their hands, and whether or not the response would show anger or emotions, they can and will use it to continue the abuse.

• **Report the cyber-bully to the local Internet service provider** ,mobile phone provider, the police, and the school. The bully's IP address can be tracked by the providers and the police. More and more schools are adopting anti-cyber-bullying policies, and even if your school has not done so yet, they should be informed of the problem so they have impetus to develop them.

Discussion Questions
1. What is cyber-bullying?
2. Have you or your friends ever been cyber-bullied?
3. Have you ever posted any personal pictures online?

Chapter 3: Effects of Bullying on Those Who Are Targeted

Children who have been the victims of bullying can suffer from long term emotional and behavioral issues. Bullying can cause depression, anxiety, and low self-esteem.

Signs to look for:
• Lack of confidence
• Nightmares
• Loss of appetite
• Depression
• Losing lunch money
• Unexplained cuts or bruises
• Poor grades

Suicide

There is evidence that bullying increases the risk of suicide. For every suicide among young people, there are at least 100 suicide attempts. Over 14% of high school students have considered suicide, and almost 7% have attempted it. Suicide is the 3rd leading cause of death among young people, resulting in about 4,400 deaths per year.

Over 14% of high school students have considered suicide, and almost 7% have attempted it. Girls between the ages of 10-14 years old may be at even greater risk of suicide. That risk goes up exponentially when the victim is taunted over sexual orientation: gay, lesbian and transgender students are far more likely to be bullied into a suicide attempt.

Bullying isn't what it used to be. Children aren't necessarily any crueler today than they were in times past—children have always found ways to taunt their peers—but children today have greater accessibility to methods of reaching their peers after the school bell rings. Home computers, cell phones, mobile gaming units like Sony's PSP, iPads and other such gadgets mean that if a child is online, there is no escape from the taunting that kids in decades past could avoid by, say, taking a different route home from school. The bullies can reach them on Facebook, Twitter, MySpace, Reddit and any number of other social networking sites. When the bullying isn't just public, but internationally public on the World Wide Web, the risk of suicide becomes greater than ever.

Preventing Suicide of Bullied Youths

How do you help a child in distress regain a healthy emotional balance and peace of mind? It isn't necessarily easy, but it is achievable and must be done if your child is going to thrive into adulthood.

If you believe that a child you know is in imminent danger of committing suicide, it is vital to seek immediate professional help. A psychiatrist, clinical therapist, counselor or other mental health professional can give you immediate access to tools that can, at the very least, relieve the urgency of the victim's emotional pain.

However, medication and counseling are only a couple of the tools available to you. Most importantly, you have your own understanding of the child's personality and emotional needs, which means that you have the power to help your child understand that his or her worth has nothing to do with other people's opinions.

Parents and caregivers can only actively prevent suicide attempts if they know that their child is in emotional turmoil. Below are several signs to watch for. If the signals below have become apparent, it is time to take immediate action.

• **A sudden change in behavior or temperament**. While there are any number of things that could cause an otherwise healthy kid to "turn on a dime" and become like someone else, such changes can be a warning sign of youthful thoughts of suicide, despondence, or drug addiction. Regardless of the reason, sudden alterations in the child's sense of self should be noted and examined.

• **An unexplained preoccupation with death.** It is perfectly normal for children to be fascinated by death after their first real experience with it, be it the loss of a grandparent, the family pet, a classmate, etc. However, an unhealthy preoccupation with morbid interests may point to a darker motive than mere curiosity. Understanding why your child holds these interests is an important step in assessing his or her emotional health.

• **Preparing "final arrangements" for their pets or belongings.**
If a child you know is writing out a will or suddenly giving away cherished possessions, something is going on to disturb the child's emotional state. Though it is a terrifying notion for any parent to consider, this is a major sign that a child or teenager feels he or she has nothing to live for. Ask them why they suddenly feel the need to rid themselves of their belongings. If you are lucky, the child could simply be caught up in something like the "tiny house" movement or a similar environmental concern about consumerism and waste. If your child indicates that he "won't need these things soon," get immediate mental health care from a qualified professional.

• **Suicide threats**. There is a terrible misconception that people who intend to kill themselves won't talk about it; but that simply isn't true. Many people — suicidal youth included — will express their feelings of despair through either verbal or non-verbal means. They may write a suicide note, but tell you it's just a poem if they are confronted about it. They may make direct or indirect statements to the effect of having nothing to live for or a longing to die. If you hear or see any such threats of suicide (especially when combined with other signs), take them seriously: They may be nothing more than a budding Goth phase, or they may be indicators that the child is seriously contemplating removing themselves from this world. That's not a risk any parent should be willing to take.

What do you do if you suspect your child is contemplating suicide? Below are some vital steps you can take to gain some understanding of the situation and how to best help your child cope:

• **First, don't freak out.** Simply ask the child directly whether he or she is contemplating suicide. Regardless of the answer, if you feel that he or she is in danger of self-harm, discreetly remove any items from the home that could likely be used in a suicide attempt.

• **Listen to anything that they have to tell you** without judgment and with a constant focus of concern for the child. If you start judging or throwing around accusations, you will effectively shut off a vital line of communication. You want your child to be able to talk to you.

• **Help them to understand that the overwhelming emotions** that they are feeling are temporary, and that they will change as the child grows and learns to see things from different perspectives. Helping your child look at the world through a different framework and showing them how to turn a situation from a negative to a positive is an important step that any parent or guardian can take to stabilize the child's emotional health.

• **Make an appointment with a mental health professional.** Your child may resent you for making them go to counseling or take prescription psychiatric medications in the short-term, but the end result — an emotionally healthy, stable and ALIVE adult — is worth it.

Discussion Questions
1. Ask your child, have you ever contemplated suicide?
2. Have you or your friends ever discussed suicide?
3. If your child was emotionally overwhelmed, would they feel comfortable talking to you?

Chapter 4: Encourage Your Child to Speak to an Adult

Children who are victims of bullying will usually keep this information to themselves for fear of repercussions. This is not ideal since we live in a society where bystanders usually don't speak up or stand up for the victim.

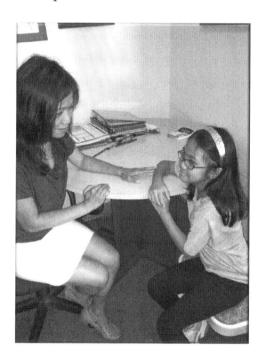

Parents should take the initiative to encourage their child to tell someone in charge when they happen to be a victim, or witness a bullying incident. From the child's point of view, this is easier said than done. Occurrences of bullying almost always go undetected until something devastating happens to bring the incident to light. It's very uncommon for the victim to tell on the bully for fear of being ridiculed. Parents need to emphasize that bullying in any manner is unacceptable. The best way to get your child to speak up, should they encounter a bullying experience, is to reassure them through constant communication, support, and training.

Parents should be aware of their home environment and how this impacts their child's confidence and ability to speak up. When a child doesn't feel safe, supported, or their opinions matter, then that becomes an acceptable standard for how they are treated outside the home.

Adults should be on the alert for children who seem to have the potential to be a bully. Victims are encouraged to tell on the bully until the aggressive behavior is eliminated altogether.

Discussion Questions
1. Ask your child: If they were being bullied who would they tell?
2. If they witnessed someone being bullied, what would they do?
3. Have any of your friends demonstrated the potential to be a bully?
4. Who are your friends at school? (In your class)
5. What is your favorite game/activity on the playground?

6. Is everyone playing together? Is there anyone that is annoying or bothersome?
7. Are there any new students? Are they by themselves? Did you invite them to play with you?

Chapter 5: Insist on School Officials Immediate Intervention

It is advised not to go directly to the bully or their parent in a school related incident. Speak to the proper school officials to keep this situation from escalating out of control. Insisting on the school officials' immediate intervention would be the best way to handle this matter. When there is persistent bullying, do not take this situation into your own hands. In almost all documented cases, the end results were tragic.

From the victim's point of view, this may not be the best solution. The child would be worried about the possible repercussions from the bully. Here the parent would have to take extra measures to ensure the identity of the child is not revealed. The parent should insist the school take the utmost care in handling the matter swiftly and effectively. All contact with school officials should be documented. This will help you in the event that there is insufficient action on the part of the school. Your child's well-being is at stake, so don't take this lightly. Your job is to protect your child. In some situations, legal action may be necessary. Having properly documented all interactions will help you support your case.

The initial step in the school's method for dealing with bullying will usually be to get all relevant information involving the case. Once a bullying situation has been verified, schools will often use suspension or other serious consequences to ensure that the bully understands the severity of his or her actions.

Discussion Questions
1. Has your child approached a school official for any reason? If so, what was the result?
2. Do you have the proper contact information for the appropriate school officials?

Chapter 6: Seek a Balance Between Solo and Group Activities

Children who are unable to get along with others in a group will eventually be an ideal target for bullies. Parents should take it upon themselves to teach children to participate in group activities in order to develop social skills. These activities will be beneficial and foster togetherness.

Solo activities such as shooting hoops, skateboarding, art, reading, and computer games can help develop a child's independence. Seeking a balance between solo and group activities is important to your child's development.

Another key factor is teaching your child how to make friends. In my academy we are very deliberate about teaching this valuable skill. When a child learns how to interact with others, they automatically increase their confidence and are less likely to become isolated. You can read more about teaching this skill to your child in the next chapter on confidence.

Discussion Questions
1. Who do they play with at recess?
2. What kind of activities do they participate in at recess?
3. Who do they eat lunch with?

Chapter 7: Teaching Confidence

It is a fact that bullies often target people they can easily intimidate. When a child is taught how to face situations with composure and confidence, then they are less likely to be the victim of bullying.

It is my belief that bullying will never go away. I believe the true answer to the bullying issue is to instill confidence in our children. Confidence cannot be taught; confidence must be learned through experience. Just because you understand what confidence is, doesn't mean you have it. It's not enough to learn what it is — you actually have to experience it, to become it. So you can't teach it, but you can provide an experience where the child can have a feeling of confidence.

Children learn through games and stories. These can be helpful tools, but what we have found to be the most effective method is to role-play with your child. When your child role-plays, they are simulating the experience in a safe environment. Similar to practicing martial arts techniques in the classroom, you must practice until the habit is formed and the response becomes automatic. This is what we call word vs. world lessons. A word lesson is when someone explains something to you and you understand, but a world lesson is when you experience it for yourself. For example, if I were to ask you to describe what it's like to bite into an apple you might find it difficult to explain. However, if you bit into an apple then you would have the personal experience.

Here are some additional techniques that will assist you in instilling confidence in your child.

• **Give them permission** and let them know when it is ok to defend themselves.

• **Teach them how to act or behave** in bullying situations, then support them when it   happens.

• **Stay in constant communication**.

• **Use positive affirmations**. An example of this is using "you can do it" statements rather than "that's not the way you do it!"

• **Never compare your child to another child**. Your child may feel superior or inferior; either way, this will not lead to a healthy self-esteem. Statements like, "Why can't you be more like your brother?" or "You can't do anything right," should be avoided.

•**Positive reinforcement**: Respond to the child with "great work" or a high five when they do something well.

•**Think about what you want the child to do versus what not to do.**
For example: If you want the child to walk, say "walk" instead of "don't run"; If a child has a tendency to hit say, "hands to yourself " versus "don't hit".

Note: For more information on effective parenting techniques, I recommend Thomas Gordon's book, P.E.T.

Now that you have some tools for instilling confidence, let me give you some ideas on how to effectively teach your child to overcome bullying.

• **Awareness:** Teaching your child to assess the situation before taking any action would be the first step. Teaching your child the art of trusting their instincts will also help them when they are trying to figure out the situation at hand. Give them examples of different situations and ask them to demonstrate what they would do. Include various scenarios that could happen in the playground, classroom, school bus, and the lunchroom.

• **Breathing**: Teaching your child proper breathing skills will allow them to stay calm in any situation. Again, this should be practiced until they don't have to think about it. Make sure that you teach them how to use slow, deep, relaxed breaths from the diaphragm. Teach them how the combination of posture and breath can demonstrate confidence.

• **Communication skills:** Keeping a cool head and speaking in a confident tone will help to deflect any immediate threat from a bully. It should be noted that any action taken on the part of the victim should not be done in a manner that might be perceived as trying to challenge the bully. This could create a negative outcome and the victim could eventually end up being blamed for the whole situation. Standing one's ground with an air of composure, despite the actual feeling of fear, should be something the parent encourages the child to practice. In addition, children should learn how to communicate and create rapport. This will be a valuable tool that will last a lifetime.

Here are some pointers on techniques to develop effective communication and rapport skills:

• **Name times three theory**. Use a person's name three times in your conversation. It will help you to remember their name and it personalizes your message.

• **Be the first to initiate conversation**. Be friendly and outgoing. Be willing to introduce yourself to others. This will help you make friends.

• **Develop a great hand shake**. This is a skill that will last you a lifetime. Having a great handshake is the first step to gaining trust.

• **Speak slowly and be heard**. The faster you speak, the less people will understand you. In addition to speaking slowly, make sure you speak at the appropriate volume, this will demonstrate confidence.

• **Discuss, don't argue**. The purpose of having conversations is to exchange ideas and information. A good communicator explains calmly what they believe in.

• **Focus on the person speaking**. To be a good communicator, focus on the response of the people you are talking to. Read their body language, this will tell you how they feel about what you are saying.

• **Learn to listen**. It is said that we have one mouth and two ears because we should listen twice as much as we speak. Allow others to speak without interruption. Listen closely to what they have to say.

• **Develop rapport-building skills**. One of the best ways to build rapport is to be interested in, and express a sense of curiosity about, other people. Ask questions about what a person is saying, and when they answer, ask a question about their answer.

• **Develop eye contact while communicating**. Making eye contact with people when you are talking demonstrates confidence. Eye contact suggests that you are interested and want to continue the conversation.

• **Never forget to smile**. It takes more muscles to frown (47) than it does to smile (17). Smiling is a sign of being open to communication and welcoming people.

• **Repeat back what was said**. Before you respond to what someone is saying, repeat back to them what you heard. This way, there will be no misunderstanding about what was said.

Despite your best efforts, sometimes a bullying situation can escalate.

Here are some tips your child can use when confronted.

•**Distance**: Teach them to keep their distance. In teaching self-defense and martial arts skills we know that the person who controls the distance controls the situation. When approached, they should step back, keep their hands up and open in a stop-like gesture. Posture should be straight; maintain eye contact. Your child may be able to gain confidence by observing themselves in a mirror so they can see the positive visual effects.

•**Exits:** Teach your child to be aware of exits and what is available to them in their environment. Knowing where they are in relationship to their environment can be very beneficial in any situation. Play the exit game; see if they can identify where the exits are when you are out with them.

• **Get away**: Teach your child to get away. Let them know that there is nothing wrong with getting away from a dangerous situation. Let them know what they should do once they get away, where they should go, who they should contact.

• **Fight back:** This should be a last resort. Teach them to seek every way possible to resolve conflict with their words before ever resorting to physical action. If all else fails, then they may be left with no choice. Practice different scenarios with them, see how they respond and correct them accordingly. This is where working in conjunction with their martial arts instructor would be especially beneficial.

Discussion Questions
1. What is confidence?
2. What is the most effective way to instill confidence in your child?
3. What is a word versus a world lesson?
4. Do I as a parent compare my child to other children?
5. What are the most important communication and rapport building skills for your child?

Chapter 8: Martial Arts Training

The training at most self-defense academies does not promote the use of violence; however, having knowledge of self-defense will be useful in building your child's confidence.

If the primary reason for enrolling your child in a martial arts academy is to have them learn how to defend themselves, the parent should make this clear to the instructor.

A child should never brag or show off that they have knowledge of self- defense. This can incite trouble and should not be encouraged.

There are several benefits of martial arts training that can be realized, one of which is the ability to improve one's physical condition. A child who is physically active will be less likely to be the target of a bully. A study done at the University of Michigan and published in the Journal of Pediatrics, showed that young children who are obese or overweight, are 60% more likely to be bullied than other children in their age group. A 2003 survey reported 13.5% of high school students are obese. Overall obesity reported in high school boys was 17.3%, nearly double the rate in girls, which was 9.4%.

When your child joins a martial arts program, there will be some level of physical fitness training such as jumping jacks, crunches, high knees, and push-ups, etc. In addition to the conditioning done in the class, I suggest playing sports with your child as well as practicing the martial arts skills learned at home. If your child is physically active and is still struggling with their weight, I suggest you consult a nutrition expert. Before starting any physical fitness program you should consult with your physician.

Another benefit of martial arts training is improved self-esteem. Having good self-esteem is a good deterrent to bullying.

The child should understand when it would be appropriate to use self- defense skills. This is a discussion we encourage all parents to have with their children. To ensure some level of safety when being confronted by a bully, self-defense techniques should be practiced until they are performed automatically when threatened.

Choosing the Right Martial Arts Academy

Not all martial arts academies are alike. What makes some martial arts academies different is simply that a child doesn't have to be the best; they just have to do their best.

If a high degree of focus is put on the physical nature of martial arts in the classroom, we're not helping children develop at an intellectual and emotional level. In my academy, we have a simple teaching philosophy, "character first, ability second." Ability takes time to develop, in most cases years, with countless hours of repetition and discipline. Character is something we can all develop in a short period of time. It's through the perfection of character that students will develop the ability to stick to their training and develop the skills required.

Let me give you a parallel for the adult world. If you want to maintain a high degree of physical fitness, you have to work out. That doesn't mean you have to over-exert yourself each and every time you go to the gym. You just have to do your best while you're at the gym. Over time you will learn to enjoy working out, develop discipline from pushing yourself, and increase your confidence as you see the difference in your physical appearance.

The process of learning martial arts is similar. You simply focus on doing your best.

When choosing the right academy for your child, consider the following:

• Do they offer a free trial lesson? This way you can see how your child will be taught and ask questions about the academy's teaching philosophy.

• Can you, as the parent, participate in at least the free trial lesson with your child? This will give you the experience from the student's perspective. Ask yourself, do you feel empowered after taking the lesson? If not, your child won't either.

• What is expected of you as a parent in the academy? Do they encourage parental involvement, support, and practice at home with your child?

• Don't base your decision to enroll your child solely on price or convenience, instead focus on the quality of the instruction and the rapport of the instructor with you and your child.

• How long is the basic agreement and can it be canceled?

• What is your flexibility level versus your commitment level? Are you willing to modify your child's activity schedule to suit the academy's class schedule?

• Ask if your child has to participate in tournaments. The tournament experience can be good, but only when the time is right. Tournaments may not be a good experience for all children.

• What are your goals for your child in studying martial arts? Make sure that your goals can be accomplished in the academy of your choice.

• Martial arts are based on eastern philosophy. Are you in agreement with the protocol of the academy?

• Once your child has accomplished the basic level of training, support their efforts to continue training. You will find that accomplishing the goal of earning a black belt will make a tremendous difference in your child's life.

Discussion Questions
1. When is it appropriate to use self-defense?
2. Have a discussion with your child about fitness and nutrition.

Chapter 9: Basic Self-Defense Techniques

Now let's discuss and review some basic martial arts techniques. These techniques are covered in most martial arts classes. For the purpose of this book we will begin with fundamental techniques for blocking, striking, kicking, and stance work. In the following chapter, we will bring it all together by demonstrating "what if " scenarios. We will look at countering assaults such as wrist grabs, bear hugs, lapel grabs, and a headlock.

Note: *This is not a self-defense course, nor is it intended to replace one. Self-defense techniques are best taught by properly trained instructors in an appropriate setting such as a gym or dojo. It is only suggestive of the very basics of actual self-defense courses. We accept no liability for any injuries that may be sustained by practicing or physically using these techniques.*

Blocks

These are defensive techniques used to stop an aggressor's strike.

Overhead block: To perform this block, start with your hand at your waist. Now move your hand until it is in front and above your head, with the palm side of your fist facing out. Your arm should be at a 45-degree angle, like a rooftop.

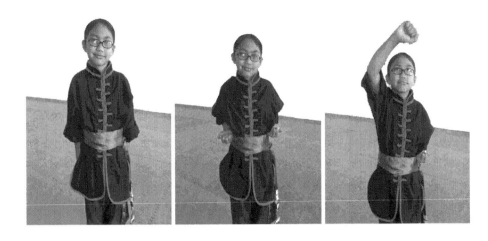

Inward block: Right from where your hand is, drop your hand to ear level, palm out, thumb to ear, now bring your arm in front to the center of your body. Your arm should be at a 45-degree angle with your fist as high as your eyebrow, palm side of fist facing you.

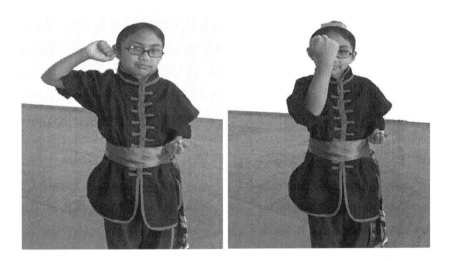

Outward block: Move your hand towards the outside of your body keeping your elbow at the same level, with your fist closed. Your palm will face out.

Downward block: Move your arm across your body and turn your palm to face you as a cat washing its face with its paw, moving past your opposite shoulder stopping at your centerline. End with your hand in front of your groin and arm away from your body.

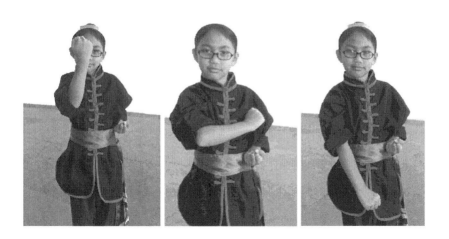

Now repeat the blocks with the other hand . . .

Strikes

There are a variety of hand techniques. We will cover just a few generic strikes in this section.

Palm strike: There are several methods of using a palm strike. The one we are using here is with the side of the palm. Make sure to pull back on wrist and strike with the edge of your hand, thrust palm straight out.

Chop: The chop should start at the ear, using the side of your hand, palm facing up as if holding a tray; bring arm swiftly to the center of your body.

Basic Punch: In traditional martial arts, the punch comes from the waist for maximum power.

Start with fists at your waist, palms facing up, as you extend your arm, turn hand over and focus on the first two knuckles.

Kicks

Kicks can be a great equalizer in self-defense when used correctly. Kicks can keep an opponent at a distance. Practice kicking at different heights. For self-defense, never kick above the waist.

Front kick: Standing with your feet shoulder width apart, lift knee towards your chest, thrust leg forward, with toes curled back. The striking point should be the ball of your foot.

Side Kick: From the same starting position, lift your knee, bringing your foot to the inside of the knee of your supporting leg. Now extend your leg to the side, striking with the outer edge of your foot.

Stances

The stances presented here will help you to have balance and strength when performing self-defense techniques.

Horse stance: The horse stance is a great stance to work your leg strength. Start with your hands on your waist. Now step out so the inside of your knees are directly below the elbows, legs should be parallel to the ground, and feet turned in.

Forward stance: The forward stance allows for use of both the lead and rear hand and foot. To begin, step forward with one foot, placing it in front of you with the front foot turned in. Your lead leg should be parallel to the ground and rear leg should be fully extended, pushing your rear foot into the ground.

Chapter 10: Self-Defense Scenarios

When all else fails and you have exhausted all other measures, self-defense becomes the only option. When your child is confronted while walking home and the bully is now taking things to a physical level and not backing down, your child must fight back or run the risk of serious injury.

Hopefully, you have used the above techniques to prepare your child with confidence. Keep in mind that even the most confident person, when physically confronted, will have some feelings of fear, especially if they don't know what to do. That's why an important part of confidence training is teaching children what to do in a self-defense situation.

Note: *The following techniques are not a complete self-defense course, nor are they intended to replace one. Self-defense techniques are best taught by properly trained instructors in an appropriate setting such as a gym or dojo. They are only suggestive of the most basic of self-defense techniques. We accept no liability for any injuries that may be sustained by practicing or physically using these techniques.*

Defense against same side wrist grab: First make your hand into a fist, then turn your wrist until your fist faces ground, then step back with the opposite leg, pulling your arm as you step back. Once your hand is released, get away as fast as you can.

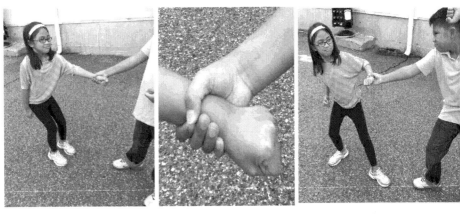

If the situation is more serious, you can follow with a chopping strike. Once you release your arm, pull all the way back to your ear, then move your arm towards opponent with palm down, strike should be made with side of hand.

Defense against a bear hug: We will work on two examples here; one from behind and the other from the front.

Opponent grabs you from behind; your arms are pinned at your sides: Drop your weight as in horse stance. (This will make it difficult for your opponent to lift you off the ground.) As you drop, raise both elbows up. Once your arms are free, drive your elbow straight back into opponent. Once the hold is broken, get away.

Grabbed from the front: Grab your own wrist and make your arms into the shape of a picture frame; then step back into forward stance and drive forearm into opponent's neck area. Once hold is broken, get away.

Defense against a lapel grab: We will look at both single hand and 2 handed attacks.

Single hand lapel grab: Opponent grabs you with one hand, pushing you backwards. Don't resist, go with it by stepping back into your horse stance. At the same time, counter-grab their grabbing hand. Now deliver an inward block to opponents elbow, follow with a palm strike to the face and get away.

Two handed lapel grab: If opponent grabs with 2 hands, reach over their arms with one hand and grab their hand. Pin both their arms to your body by dropping your arm as you step back into horse stance, raise free hand as if ringing a bell, drop elbow on crease of arms, then elbow to face, and get away.

Defense against a headlock: This attack is more serious than some of the others, because there is a risk of being choked.

When your opponent applies a headlock, first turn your head into his (or her) armpit to get air, drive your knee into his calf muscle, then go back to horse stance. Now deliver a double hammer fist strike, one to the front of the opponent and the other to the back of the opponent. Reach over opponent's shoulder and pull their head back, then follow with a palm strike and, as always, get away.

Discussion Questions
•What are the different blocks? When would you use them?
•What are the different kicks? When would you use them?
•What is the purpose of stances?
•What other scenarios can I use these techniques for?
(For example: On a school bus, in the lunch room, etc.)

Note: *Remember, you can't learn martial arts from a book! I encourage you to seek out professional instruction at a martial arts school.*

Chapter 11: Conclusion

The ideas I have shared with you will assist you in your quest to help your child deal with bullying. Besides teaching your child the communication and mental skills presented here, it is my belief that the most important attribute you can instill in your child is a sense of confidence. I encourage you to seek the advice of a trained martial arts professional, and communication and leadership experts.

Believe it or not, the one essential quality of having confidence can defuse most bullying situations before they start. Whether the confidence comes from safety in numbers, knowing that they can safely tell an adult, or that they can defend themselves, it will show in many ways, from the obvious to the subtle, and makes it clear that they will not be easily victimized.

If your child lacks personal confidence, bullies will tend to pick up on that immediately, and make them their next victim. For the most part, bullies only seek to intimidate those they see as weaker than themselves—bullying behavior, both social and physical, is all geared toward that end. It stands to reason then, that building confidence is the key element to making all the other measures that we've mentioned work.

If your child has firmly ingrained confidence, many bullies will simply leave them alone. Some may be a bit testier and try to intimidate your child at first, but will give up after it becomes obvious your son or daughter will not be pushed over so easily by their actions. It will be only in very rare cases that a bully will actually escalate to physical violence or extreme social humiliation in order to gain dominance, especially if your child is known to be confident and to be able to stand up to bullies. Violent situations or extreme humiliation, for the most part, is what bullies inflict on people they already have under their control.

Once it becomes well known at school, the neighborhood, or on the favored social media sites that your child or children are not easy targets, they will, over time, be left alone by the bullies. When your son or daughter realizes that they don't have to take lesser abuse to prevent worse bullying and that it's not a rite of passage to joining the "in crowd," a bully is much less likely to torment them.

This single quality — confidence — has a synergistic relationship with all the other things we have discussed. Confidence is present in everything we've discussed, and empowers everything. Think of it this way: The "new kid in town" is either going to be popular right from the start or they are going to be an outcast. Their self-confidence and outgoingness are going to affect what other people think. If they are confident, they will make friends and gain the societal support structure to protect them from bullies. If they merely "put on a front," but aren't really confident in themselves, they could lose those friends quickly when their mask of false confidence falls off.

In the "kids vs. adults" mentality among older children and teens, your son or daughter will have to have confidence that they can approach you with their problems. You not only have to prove to them that you will listen and not dismiss their problems, but that you will do something to fix it, such as contacting the school officials.

This also engenders trust in other adults. If your child sees how contacting the school officials fixed the problem, they will be more likely to speak to the school officials themselves. If they are led to believe that things will get worse if they tell, or if you confront the bully and mishandle the situation, things will not improve, your child will suffer in silence, and the bullying can become disastrous very quickly.

The same thing holds true with self-defense. Practice makes perfect, mainly because it builds confidence. Whether or not their technique is sloppy, self- defense can fail miserably if they are not confident in their ability to defend themselves. In one instant of self-doubt, their mind can freeze and their body will freeze also. Fear takes over, what they know of self-defense is gone with the wind, and they become the victim, regardless of how excellent they normally are in class. Confidence is everything.

 While you, yourself, may not be able to teach them public speaking, social skills or how to fight, you can definitely help build their confidence by positively encouraging them to learn these tools and how they work. Training in those areas can always be delegated to professionals, but the one thing that no professional can provide is parental support, encouragement, and, above all, communication. After all, if you don't know what they are dealing with, you can't help them. If you can't help them, then who can?

We strongly encourage taking the lessons further than the scope of this book. We have provided the core essentials of self-defense and confidence building here, but there is much more to learn out there. Think of the practices in this book as sprouting the seeds of confidence in your child.

By themselves, the practices can also help the flower of confidence grow into full blossom. However, we recognize that this single presentation of "The Self-Confidence Factor" does not cover everything that comes with a larger curriculum. With an expanded education featuring the principles of "The Self-Confidence Factor" at the center, your child's new sense of well-being can express itself in new and vibrant ways.

More important even than encouraging them to learn from this book and expand their practices by taking classes, you should join them in this journey. Being supportive, of course, is a great help, but what children really respond to is your involvement. In fact, much of what we have presented in this book specifically calls for your involvement.

By joining in the journey, you may actually learn a few things about yourself, and you may grow as well. Everyone has room to improve their confidence. Not only will you grow closer than ever with your kids, you will also learn to be a better role model — both by learning the lessons and by showing them what is right and wrong.

In conclusion, "The Self-Confidence Factor" and the practices in it do far more than simply teach a child how to protect himself against bullies. Through the lessons taught in this book, you and your children will be building a quality that is necessary to thrive in this world — confidence.

After all, confidence has applications far beyond dealing with a schoolyard bully. In fact, life is full of situations that demand confidence:

- Job Interviews
- First Dates
- Marriage Proposals
- Meeting the In-laws
- Public Presentations
- Getting Pulled Over by the Police
- Going to Court
- and much more . . .

Think of the many opportunities that have been and could be missed due to lacking confidence. Imagine a life for your children where they have the confidence to fulfill their every desire. It is closer to reality than you think.

Bibliography

Lake Washington School District. (n.d.) Guidelines for Safe Student Electronic Communications: Phones and Other Devices in Schools, Cyber- Bullying, Texting, "Sexting", FaceBook, MySpace, and Things Parents Should Know and Do http://www.lwsd.org/school/ehs/for-parents/Pages/default.aspx

STOMP Out Bullying™ (n.d.). The Issue of Bullying: http://www. stompoutbullying.org/aboutbullying_theissue.php

Suicide Prevention Resource Center. (March 2011). Suicide and Bullying Issue Brief http://www.sprc.org/sites/sprc.org/files/library/Suicide_Bullying_Issue_Brief.pdf

http://www.bullyingstatistics.org/content/bullying-and-suicide.html

Additional Resources

A Portion of the proceeds from sales of this book will be donated to The DON'T WAIT Project® and HealthCorps®.

The DON'T WAIT Project® has launched the DON'T WAIT® to Stop Bullying campaign and is partnering with Better Actions Now for the award-winning How to Unmake A Bully video series. Students write, direct, produce, act in, and film their own videos. Through the educational components of the program, students learned to take a stand against bullying, because if they are not taking a stand against it, then they are contributing to it. How to Unmake A Bully has received numerous awards, including the Telly Award, and has received endorsements from the Kids First Coalition for Quality Children's Media and The Anti-Defamation League. The program is being used in classrooms around the world as one of the "best tools available" for anti-bullying instruction and awareness. **http://dontwaitproject.org/**

HealthCorps®' vision is to lead a nationwide movement toward a new generation of healthy young people. HealthCorps® was founded by heart surgeon and two-time Daytime Emmy Award-winning talk show host, Dr. Mehmet Oz, and his wife, Lisa, to combat the childhood obesity crisis.

HealthCorps®' mission is to implement an innovative in-school model that inspires teens to make healthier choices for themselves and their families.

HealthCorps'® national peer mentoring program spans 67 high schools in 14 states (AZ, CA, DC, DE, FL, LA, MD, MS, NJ, NY, OH, OK, OR, TX) and the District of Columbia. HealthCorps® has impacted 144,100 students and 288,200 friends and family through their work. By 2015, HealthCorps® aspires to be in 100 schools across the country and impacting students in all 50 states. Make donations at **www.healthcorps.org**

For information regarding how to find a martial arts school in your area, as well as Bully Prevention seminars, please contact Sifu Karl Romain at **sifuromain@gmail.com.**

About the Author

SIFU KARL ROMAIN

World Champion and United International Kung Fu Hall of Fame inductee Sifu Romain has been studying and training in Kung Fu for 34 years.

His television appearances include: Oprah, Dr. Oz, NBC 1st Look, The Discovery Health Channel, ESPN, Good Day New York, MSG Networks, ABC-TV News and Fox National News.

Not only is Sifu Romain a World Champion, but he also trained and mentored many students who went on to become World Champions. Two of these children went on to become the youngest ever inductees into the United International Kung Fu Hall of Fame.

Sifu Romain's clientele is very diverse. His students range in age from as young as 4 up to 80. Sifu has also trained many athletes and celebrities. In fact, Amani Toomer of the New York Giants football team continues to train with Sifu Romain.

Sifu Romain is always striving to go beyond his best. He is a World Champion athlete, successful businessman, and a teacher at heart. He is continually finding ways to inspire everyone he meets to do their best.

Sifu Romain and his team have created The "Self-Confidence Factor Bully Prevention Program". It is a comprehensive program designed to give children, parents, and teachers the ability to deal with the serious issue of bullying, using common sense and non-violent solutions. The confidence factor teaches your child to use their mental self-defense before ever considering physical action and helps them stay safe and avoid potentially dangerous situations.

Other Books by Sifu Romain:

The Shaolin Athlete

In any sport, there are good athletes, great athletes, and the best of the best. This book will help you be the best of the best in your sport. But The Shaolin Athlete is not just for the serious athlete. Everyone can learn about proper health and conditioning, both for sports and for life in The Shaolin Athlete. This is because the Kung Fu Conditioning exercises taught in The Shaolin Athlete target the body, the mind, and the spirit as a whole. The

Shaolin Athlete/Kung Fu Conditioning program is the complete fitness and health program for everyone, from the professional athlete, to the weekend warrior, to the average Jane or Joe who wants to get in better shape and live longer. Kung Fu Conditioning is for fitness, health, conditioning, and longevity. "With the help of Sifu Karl Romain I was able not only to work on my shortcomings and become a more accountable football player, but also to fall in love with the process and not just fall in love with the success. I learned to love every step that it took for me to succeed in the NFL." — Amani Toomer, former receiver for the New York Giants (Amani Toomer is featured in this book)

The Cross and the Warrior — A Black Belt Christian Leadership Program

The training program was developed by Sifu Karl Romain and Dr. G. Steve Kinnard. The goal of the program is to teach Christian leadership principles through martial arts training. This course has been developed for pre-teen and teenage boys and girls. But the course can be adapted to any age group. This book shows you how to teach inspirational leadership lessons while challenging students in martial arts training.

Legendary Longfist or Legendary Longfist — EBook version

The form presented in this book is a basic long fist set from the Northern Shaolin Long Fist system. The form itself is easy to learn, yet introduces the student to a large number of sophisticated practical applications. A careful study of the form reveals its rich content, including the following concepts: fist, palm, knee and kicking attacks, blocks and parries for various hand and foot attacks, defenses to grabbing attacks, throwing techniques, chin na (seize and control) techniques, simultaneous kick and hand strike, and simultaneous block and strike. This book is divided into two sections. The first section contains a full representation of the form as performed by renowned Master Karl Romain. The second section is a representation of various practical self-defense applications of the form. Each picture is accompanied by detailed explanatory text.

43790804R00046

Made in the USA
Middletown, DE
29 April 2019